THE
LOVE GARDEN

Dedication

This book is dedicated to my husband, Matthew, who saw me through a lens of grace and never once gave up on my heart and allowed The Lord to strengthen each of us so that we can walk in His victorious redemption. I love you most.

"And I will give you a new heart, and a new spirit I will put within you.
And I will remove the heart of stone from your flesh and give you a heart of flesh."
— Ezekiel 36:26 (ESV)

Once there was a young girl who loved The Lord with all her heart. She loved His creation, the creatures of the sea, and the beasts of the land. She loved the moon, the sun, and all of the glittery stars. She loved the rain, and most of all, she loved all the beautiful plants and flowers that grew each year.

The Lord knew how His creation spoke to her heart, so one day He took her to a beautiful field by a babbling brook tucked into a meadow that seemed so magical. He said to her, "My child, I see how you love me and worship me. I see how you know My Word and seek My heart. I love you, and I am giving you this garden."

"This land may look empty, but as you tend to it, it will grow, and this will be your love garden. It will reflect your heart for me." The young girl jumped with excitement! She envisioned all the beautiful flowers she would grow, all the birds that would come to find rest. She pictured butterflies, and she knew this garden would be a beautiful reflection of praise to her Heavenly Father whom she loved so much.

"My child this is a precious gift. I know you will do much good work here. Protect it, and be fruitful, and never stop being who I created you to be. You are precious in my sight."

The girl thanked God and went straight to work. She started to till the soil, plant seeds and water them. She pruned her plants and as the seasons passed her garden flourished in the most stunning way!

the Best
wildflower
SEEDS

Soon her garden was very lush and there was always work to be done which actually brought such joy to her heart. One day a young man came by and saw the beautiful garden. He also saw the girl was now a young woman and she was very beautiful. He asked if he could come join her. She agreed and welcomed him in.

Each day the young man was there he would ask what needed to be done, and the girl would patiently show him how to care for each plant. She would show him how to leave food for certain animals, and uproot weeds that were harming the growth of the garden. All the while she would sing praises to The Lord. She loved to sing- she was ever singing His praises.

Day after day the girl continued her act of worship by tending to her garden and patiently working long hours. But the young man grew tired of all the work and annoyed at her singing and jealous of God as he could see her love for The Lord was very great.

His jealousy turned to rage and one day he ordered her to stop singing. Stunned and afraid the girl froze- silent.

The young man screamed, "I hate this garden! You're wasting your time! You've wasted my time!" And knowing her love for him would never be greater than her love for God the young man set fire to the garden.

The young woman watched all the trees, bushes and flowers become swallowed whole by a giant blaze. There was nothing she could do. The fire grew higher and her tears flowed greater.

When the flames settled into embers she was left
with ash and soot. She looked around at the
blackened earth. She felt her heart break, ache,
and become hard. She felt so ashamed that she
let this happen to the gift The Lord had given her.
She knew she had to rebuild it. But this time she
would make it strong instead of beautiful. On
that day, the girl stopped singing.

She began by creating a large wall of stones to protect the garden from any predators. She planted trees that would have thick trunks and shrubs with thorns to protect her space. Time went by, and the garden was barren. People would walk by and ask her what she was doing, to which she would answer, "I'm building a garden to reflect my love for God." The people would whisper, "She will never grow a garden there; the earth is ruined," "There's just too much work to be done," "It just seems hopeless."

Some young men would stop and try to help but all gave up quickly when they saw the damage. The young woman's heart continued to feel hard and her faith became weak. She began to wonder if God was disappointed in her. She began to wonder if God even still cared about her.

One day, a man with a strong heart and a gentle smile came through the field and saw the thorns overgrowing the stone wall. He saw the young woman silently but violently beating the soil- attempting to move rocks and roots from the ground.

"Excuse me", the strong man said "You look like you could use some help. May I lend a hand?" Discouraged from all who had given up before, the young woman barked, "No- I'm fine! I can do it myself"... The strong man asked, "May I ask, what are you doing?"

The girl threw down her shovel from and yelled, "I'm building a garden! It's meant to be strong- to reflect my love for The Lord." The strong man asked, "Why are you doing this alone?"

The question made the girl feel broken. "Because... It's helpless! This earth has been torched and has been barren for years. Only thorns grow here now- nobody has been able to help rebuild it."

The strong man saw her outer beauty, but was struck by the deep sadness in her eyes. He too loved The Lord, so he spoke up and said, "Well you seem like you know what you're doing;; may I at least help you move that heavy rock?" The girl nodded. He came beside her and lifted the weight of the boulder and let her guide him to where she wanted it, "Right here," she said, "on the wall- it needs to be taller".

The strong man gently replied, "Well, I know you want the walls taller, but it seems like these stones are keeping the water from the babbling brook. That water could carry in here and bring new life to some of the plants."

The young woman was afraid to take away the stones. She was afraid of what could come into the garden. So she said, "The earth is dead- what could possibly grow here?" The strong man smiled and said, "Actually, a lot! This soil can now serve as compost and because of the time that has passed between growth the earth below it is extremely rich in minerals."

The young woman looked puzzled and couldn't help but feel hopeless. She thought her garden was a lost cause, yet out of fear and obligation she continued to work it- but to no avail.

But could what this man be saying be true? Could her garden be saved? Could it be beautiful again?

The strong man said to her, "It's your choice, but if you trust me I can help you clear those thorns and pull the weeds and if you so choose, I can help you restore this garden." Hesitant, the young woman stopped, and replied, "Ok, but I'm not sure it's much use."

And so it began. Each morning the young woman would wake up and the strong man was already hard at work removing thick sharp thorny vines, and hauling away the large stones one by one. The strong man never seemed to grow weary, and he never seemed to lose hope. He would hum as he worked. He would work with focus and rest in the shade and she would hear him whisper. She wondered what it could be he was saying. Was he frustrated with the work? Did he feel like giving up?

Day by day the strong man made gentle suggestions. He'd say, "I'm not sure if you realize but because of the wall's height there are large shadows cast on the garden and it's stopping this area from growing at all."

The young woman was fearful of removing the wall and the strong man could tell, so he comforted her by saying, "I still think it's wise to protect this garden but maybe I can make a picket fence to be a form of protection but still let the sunshine and water in, and allow others to see its beauty. Would that be ok?" The young woman paused, and couldn't think of anything wrong with that, but her heart was still hard, so she answered, "Yes but stay on the outside of the garden as you build it.", "Of course," he replied.

Each sunrise and sunset came with more toil for the strong man but he kept a gentle spirit and a joyful heart. He continued to hum while he worked and would whisper while he rested, sometimes with his eyes closed, and sometimes with his eyes facing the warm sun.

Every day brought more light into the garden and the promise of hope started to grow in the young woman's heart.

On a cool morning the young woman awoke and did not see the strong man at work. She felt her heart sink. She knew it! It was too much work; it was too far gone; it wasn't worth the effort. She felt hopeless again.

Just then, in the distance, the morning fog lifted and she saw the strong man walking towards her with large beams of wood in his arms. He smiled grandly at her and said, "Good morning! I was hoping I could share something with you!"

The young woman felt relief and surprise and stood very still- she could not believe he was still there. "What is it?", she asked as her heart began to beat quickly. "This morning while I was praying I felt The Lord remind me of His call upon your life to rest in Him. It was like the Holy Spirit was saying, 'She needs a Selah- she needs to rest and abide in Me', so I was hoping you would allow me to build you a bench where you can rest inside of your garden?"

The strong man stood there with hope and excitement in his eyes and the young woman felt the hard walls around her heart begin to pierce and crack every so slightly.

He had been praying for her? "You- you prayed for me?" she stuttered. "Of course!" he chuckled, "I pray all day long! As I work, I worship. I always need to go back to The Father to ask what He needs of me and what the next right step of obedience is. He is the great shepard, He leads me to paths of righteousness."

It was then that she realized that that was his humming and whispering. It was his worship and prayer to The Lord. It had been so long since she had felt praise spring from inside her, that in that moment she felt a freedom break loose inside her. "Well?", he smiled, "these beams are a little heavy, if you'd like I can start on the bench right away!" The young woman nodded excitedly, and the two went to work for the day.

As the afternoon sun rose higher and the clouds parted she felt the warmth of the suns rays touch her cheek, and she lifted her eyes from the dark earth for the first time in years. She breathed slowly and watched the birds glide gently in the sky. Just then, she felt her heart flutter with a tune. She started to hum as she continued to work- and the day felt different; she felt stronger.

As time passed and the earth turned into beautiful lush soil for the most vibrant exotic flowers, the young woman's hum became a song again. She started noticing the butterflies returning to her side, and the sun showers brought the most vibrant rainbows. She saw God's grace and creation all around her. Her garden was even more beautiful than she had ever dreamed and her heart grew fuller with songs of praise for The Lord.

One afternoon, when the ornate bench had been finished, the strong man stood on the outside of the white picket fence and said, "I have your bench here, if you'd like I can bring it to you, if you'll allow me to come in and see what you have created."

The woman smiled. He had never pushed or forced, never shown impatience. He had been full of discipline and grace and kept his focus on The Lord and led with gentleness and peace. She opened the gate for him and he lifted the bench inside. He had so carefully and meticulously crafted it to be a beautiful sturdy piece of her garden.

He sat the bench down in the shade of a blossoming tree and took the young woman by the hand and said, "What you have built here to reflect your heart for The Lord is so mighty and brilliant and will last for generations and be a blessing to others." He paused then said, "I have this for you."

He pulled out a lock and key from his back pocket, "The fence will allow others to see and witness this beauty but I heard from The Lord that you still need to guard what He has given you, so I fashioned you a strong lock with a key, and this is the one and only key so that you will forever feel safe in this place of worship."

The young woman had tears flow from her eyes, and a rushing feeling in her spirit as her heart burst open like a flood. She felt gratitude, hope, peace, strength... She felt seen and safe. She put her hand on the lock and closed her eyes and thanked The Lord and heard Him whisper to her heart, "He is wise, he is strong, and you can trust him my sweet child. Be free."

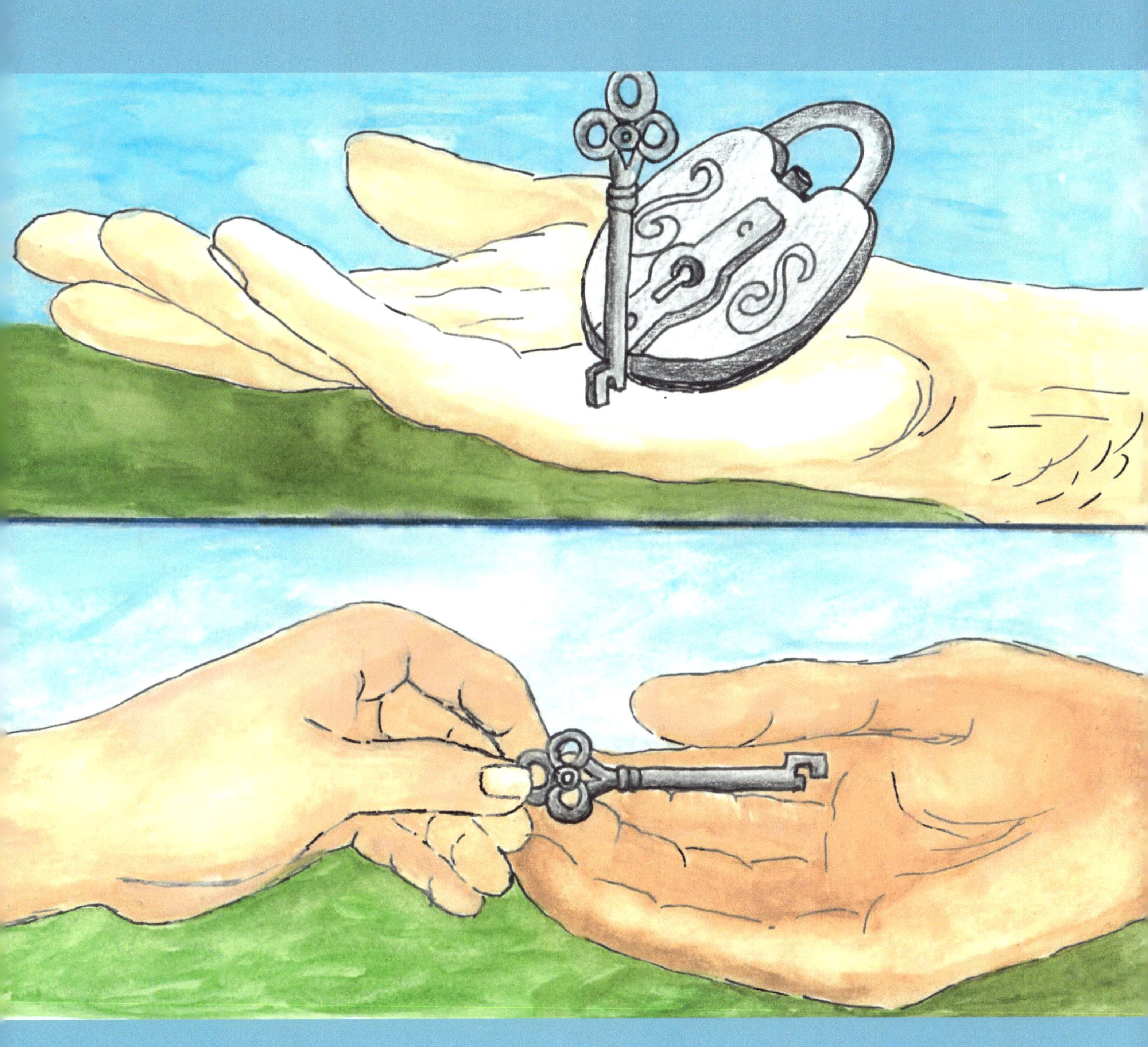

The strong man stood tall, and leaned in patiently while the young woman felt relief for the first time in years. She placed the key back in hand and folded his fingers around it and said. "This garden, like the song in my heart, will forever sing the praises of our God. He has redeemed what once seemed so far gone. I trust Him with my life, and He has shown me that you are the one to share this with. You and only you."

The strong man held her and said, "Together, we can magnify The Lord and exalt His name, as long as we both shall live." And that is exactly what they did, all the days of their life.

"And I will give you a new heart, and a new spirit I will put in you. And I will remove the heart of stone from you and give you a heart of flesh."
-Ezekiel 36:26 (ESV)